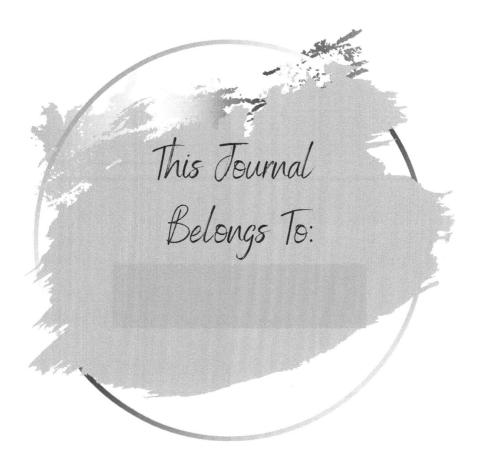

This Journal

Belongs To:

Writing Prompts:

What made you smile today and why?

What are you grateful for and why?

Describe the best thing that happened to you today.

What are 5 things that you would advise your younger self and why?

Where do you see yourself in 5 years? 10 years?

How are you expressing your creativity?

What does resiliency mean to you and why?

Writing Prompts:

How are you uniquely different from others?

What does success look like to yoy and why?

How are you being a better person today than you were yesterday?

Let's S.W.O.T it out! What are your strengths, weaknesses, opportunities and threats?

How is social media impacting you in a positive way and why?

What books, podcasts, tutorials and more resonate with your current well-being and why?

How are you developing your goals and shifting your mindset?

Writing Prompts:

What does wellness look like to you? Why?

What are 5 must haves for a healthy relationship? Do you see those things within your networks?

How can self-care impact your well-being?

Who are the most important people in your life and why?

What are the next 5 steps that you need to make to improve your success?

What are 10 things that you love about yourself and why?

How can you impact your community and why?

INSTAGRAM:
@CURLS_COILS
@WORDS_WINEFESTMD

SCAN IT!

CLUBHOUSE:
@CURLS_COILS

FACEBOOK:
@CURLSCOILSMD

Made in the USA
Coppell, TX
28 August 2022